D1712824

SHINGYŌ

REFLECTIONS ON TRANSLATING THE HEART SUTRA

M.J. SULLIVAN
SEIHŌ

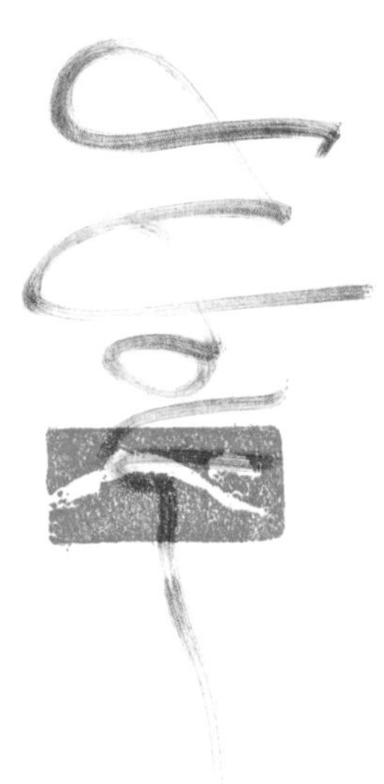

Shingyō: Reflections on Translating the Heart Sutra.

By: M.J. Sullivan (Seihō)

Revised 2018

ISBN 978-0-9829920-3-6
Library of Congress Control Number 2012955188

1.Japanese-English translation. 2. Heart Sutra. 3. Zen Buddhist Meditation.
4. Japanese Calligraphy. 5. Asian Languages.

I Title.

For further information, address:

Silverback Sages, Publishers, L.L.C.
P. O. Box 1408
Abiquiu, New Mexico 87510.

SILVERBACK SAGES

FIVE CALLIGRAPHIC VERSIONS

OF THE

SHINGYŌ

所得故菩提薩埵依般若波羅蜜多故心无
罣礙无罣礙故无有恐怖遠離一切顛倒夢
想究竟涅槃三世諸佛依般若波羅蜜多故
得阿耨多羅三藐三菩提故知般若波羅蜜
多是大神咒是大明咒是无上咒是无等等
咒能除一切苦真實不虛故說般若波羅蜜
多咒即說咒曰
揭諦揭諦 波羅揭諦 波羅僧揭諦 菩提薩婆訶

辛卯年文月

聖峯謹書

心経

觀自在菩薩行深般若波羅蜜多時照見五

蘊皆空度一切苦厄舍利子色不異空空不

異色色即是空空即是色受想行識亦復如

是舍利子是諸法空相不生不滅不垢不淨

不增不減是故空中无色无受想行識无眼

耳鼻舌身意无色聲香味觸法无眼界乃至

无意識界无无明亦无无明盡乃至无老死

亦无老死盡无苦集滅道无智亦无得以无

The Sumidera Shingyō
Nara Period, Kyoto National Museum
Copy by Seihō, 2010

罣礙無罣礙故無有恐怖遠離一切顛倒夢
想究竟涅槃三世諸佛依般若波羅蜜多故
得阿耨多羅三藐三菩提故知般若波羅蜜
多是大神呪是大明呪是無上呪是無等等
呪能除一切苦真実不虚故説般若波羅蜜
多呪即説呪曰
羯諦羯諦 波羅羯諦 波羅僧羯諦 菩提薩婆訶
般若心経

摩訶般若波羅蜜多心経

觀自在菩薩行深般若波羅蜜多時照見五
蘊皆空度一切苦厄舍利子色不異空空不
異色色即是空空即是色受想行識亦復如
是舍利子是諸法空相不生不滅不垢不浄
不増不減是故空中無色無受想行識無眼
耳鼻舌身意無色声香味觸法無眼界乃至
無意識界無無明亦無無明尽乃至無老死
亦無老死尽無苦集滅道無智亦無得以無
所得故菩提薩埵依般若波羅蜜多故心無

The Myōshinji Shingyō
Seihō, 2011

所得故菩提薩埵依般若波羅蜜多故心無
罣礙無罣礙故無有恐怖遠離一切顛倒夢
想究竟涅槃三世諸佛依般若波羅蜜多故
得阿耨多羅三藐三菩提故知般若波羅蜜
多是大神咒是大明咒是無上咒是無等等
咒能除一切苦真實不虛故說般若波羅蜜
多咒即說咒曰
揭諦揭諦 波羅揭諦 波羅僧揭諦 菩提薩婆訶
般若心經

佛說摩訶般若波羅蜜多心經
觀自在菩薩行深般若波羅蜜多時照見五
蘊皆空度一切苦厄舍利子色不異空空不
異色色即是空空即是色受想行識亦復如
是舍利子是諸法空相不生不滅不垢不浄
不增不減是故空中無色無受想行識無眼
耳鼻舌身意無色聲香味觸法無眼界乃至
無意識界無無明亦無無明盡乃至無老死
亦無老死盡無苦集滅道無智亦無得以無

The Daikakuji Shingyō
Copy by Seihō

亦無老死盡無苦集滅道無智亦無得以無
所得故菩提薩埵依般若波羅蜜多故心無
罣礙無罣礙故無有恐怖遠離一切顛倒夢
想究竟涅槃三世諸佛依般若波羅蜜多故
得阿耨多羅三藐三菩提故知般若波羅蜜
多是大神咒是大明咒是無上咒是無等等
咒能除一切苦真實不虛故說般若波羅蜜
多咒即說咒曰
揭諦揭諦　波羅揭諦　波羅僧揭諦　菩提薩婆訶
般若心經

佛説摩訶般若波羅蜜多心経

觀自在菩薩行深般若波羅蜜多時照見五
蘊皆空度一切苦厄舎利子色不異空空不
異色色即是空空即是色受想行識亦復如
是舎利子是諸法空相不生不滅不垢不浄
不増不減是故空中無色無受想行識無眼
耳鼻舌身意無色聲香味觸法無眼界乃至
無意識界無無明亦無無明盡乃至無老死

The Kampō Shingyō
Copy by Seiho, 2011

罣礙無罣礙故無有恐怖遠離一切顛倒夢
想究竟涅槃三世諸佛依般若波羅蜜多故
得阿耨多羅三藐三菩提故知般若波羅蜜
多是大神呪是大明呪是無上呪是無等等
呪能除一切苦眞實不虚故説般若波羅蜜
多呪即説呪曰
羯諦羯諦波羅羯諦波羅僧羯諦
菩提娑婆呵
般若心經

辛卯年弥生

西峯謹書

摩訶般若波羅蜜多心經

観自在菩薩行深般若波羅蜜多時照見五
蘊皆空度一切苦厄舎利子色不異空空不
異色色即是空空即是色受想行識亦復如
是舎利子是諸法空相不生不滅不垢不浄
不増不減是故空中無色無受想行識無眼
耳鼻舌身意無色聲香味觸法無眼界乃至
無意識界無無明亦無無明盡乃至無老死
亦無老死盡無苦集滅道無智亦無得以無
所得故菩提薩埵依般若波羅蜜多故心無

The Hōsenji Shingyō
Seihō, 2011

ALSO BY M. J. SULLIVAN

Seihō's Kanji Workbook

Sword and Psyche

WAZA

Japanese Calligraphy: Practice, Learning, and Art
(with the Calligraphy of Harada Kampō)

Japanese Calligraphy: A First Year Curriculum
(with the Calligraphy of Harada Kampō)

Velvet
(with Alec Kalla)

Silk and Steel

In This Living Body

Three-Strand Cordage

SHINGYŌ

Table of Contents

Foreword

M. J. Sullivan's involvement with The Heart Sutra has stretched over many, many years. His love for the *Shingyō* spans a range of approaches, from Buddhist meditation practice and chanting, to calligraphy, and even to *Iaidō*, perhaps the most esoteric discipline of Japanese swordsmanship, using real swords. Now he offers us the fruits of his many years of study, reflection and practice, in a book that is both a work of art and a significant contribution to scholarship on the Heart Sutra. Sullivan wears his erudition lightly, but this book contains not only a distillation of scholarly literature concerning the translation of the sutra—his ostensible purpose—but also a deep engagement with hermeneutical issues around the text itself.

We are treated to fine copies of the sutra, in his own hand, that are themseles copies of earlier noteworthy copies. The main body of the book is a character by character reference work on the text—each character translated literally, but also with useful notes regarding issues that arise at critical points for any translator or reader of translations.

The book includes a brief, deeply personal essay by Sullivan on how the Heart Sutra has affected his own experience, and his grasp of the "reality" in which we live, and move and have our being.

This book will be an important resource for anyone for whom the Heart Sutra is of spiritual significance. For those of us who are not at ease with the Chinese characters themselves, Sullivan has done our "dictionary work" for us. This book will also be of interest to scholars who are engaged more deeply with the text itself. Sullivan is a reliable guide to where the trip-lines are planted.

But, above all, this lovely book is infused with Sullivan's artistic sensitivity, and his love and respect for this very important Buddhist text.

Charles W. Swain, Ph.D.
Professor of Religion (retired)
Florida State University
Tallahassee, Florida
July 17, 2012

Prologue

Takamatsu, Japan, 1979

The pre-dawn is cool and smells of trees and plants rather than of trains or traffic. The tires of my bicycle hiss on the pavement and there is a sharp squawk from one of the pedals. I find my way through the darkened streets to the Zen temple, get there five minutes before five. I rack my bike next to several others. The gate is open. I walk quickly past the tall bronze Buddha, who gazes across to the modern Prefectural ofice building with perfect equanimity. When I reach the hall I see a businessman in the flagstone vestibule removing his shoes. The sliding door to the hall is open. One or two office ladies, a college student, and a young man in a black tracksuit are sitting on pillows in one or another degree of the Lotus position or sitting on their heels. No one looks up when I enter and take a place on the tatami mat nearest the door, arrange the pillows I find there and sit. One other person enters and arranges himself across the aisle, the last one. Then silence.

I see that preparations have been made on the dais. A scroll has been hung. An arrangement of fresh flowers flanks the wooden gong and a pillow has been placed dead center of all of it. It is a pleasing picture. The scroll is large and bordered with two contrasting silk brocades framing a single character brushed boldly and wildly to fill its entire paper center. It reads *Emptiness*.

The priest enters. His head is shaved and he wears a brown robe with the strap over the soulder. He is perhaps forty. He moves smoothly to his cushion, seats himself and arranges his robes gracefully. He looks out over the rest of the hall, spots me. He nudges the woman seated nearest him, whispers. She rises, reaches behihd her for something, walks silently to me and hands me a small white pamphlet. I bow from my seat, raising the pamphlet to my forehead. She bows, returns to her seat.

The priest puts a match to the incense and soon sandalwood gently fills the air. I close my eyes and from within, not from within the me I know but from the belly of the priest, comes a sound that jolts my body, a huge, deep, penetrating sound, I sit stunned, I have heard recordings but this is entirely other than they ever were, gradually I can distinguish syllables, *Ma ka han nya ha ra mi ta shin gyō*. The *gyō* strings out in time, drops in pitch until it is a growl that disappears into my body and sticks there. Then I hear the sound of the wooden gong and the voices of all around me and I realize that this is what the pamphlet is for, I am to chant with them. I finally find my place, or think I do, but I lose the rhythm. I will have to practice, so I just listen and let the sound carry me, wherever they are going I will go.

At a point all the voices stop but that of the priest and his alone intones the last four syllables, *Han nya shin gyō*, the *gyō* again extended and dropping in pitch to a growl. Silence follows. I know what to do with that, I have learned to follow the breath, empty the mind. I meditate. We all meditate. On *Emptiness*.

Time can be just time, and space can be just space,
but some cases require a time/space continuum.

色 can be just 色, and 識 can be just 識,
but some cases require a 色/識 continuum.

Introduction

Shingyō is the Sino-Japanese pronunciation of "*Hridaya Sutra*", usually translated into English as "Heart Sutra". The Heart Sutra, the most popular of all of the Buddhist sacred texts, is said to contain the essential elements of Buddhist thought and doctrine, and to be accepted by all sects. It is chanted in many languages, and copied in hand by many calligraphers around the world. The calligraphic element has a special fascination for artists both sacred and secular. It also is of great interest as a subject of philosophical discussion.

There have been many commentaries on the Heart Sutra, most of them dealing with early versions of the text in Sanskrit and Tibetan, that is, its form *before* its translation into Chinese. (A note here: Some scholars and historians think that it was actually written in Chinese originally, and that the Sanskrit and Tibetan versions were translated *from the Chinese*, rather than the other way around. In this study, I will ignore this delightful idea, and follow the conventional wisdom. See "A Final and Fanciful Note on the Authorship of the *Shingyō*".)

All but two of the commentaries we'll mention here are of this sort, and are in English or were translated into English. These may or may not be of help in our concern here, which is to address the question of, first, what the *Shingyō* actually says in Chinese, and second, what it meant to them when they translated it from the Sanskrit and Tibetan in the second and third centuries (if indeed that was how it went).

Why would we want to know about this? Isn't it enough that we have translations, some most authoritative, from the Sanskrit and Tibetan? I submit that there are good reasons. Sanskrit and Tibetan are written in phonetics. Chinese is ideographic in its written form, so that we don't have to know how it sounds (or once sounded) in Hindi, Urdu, Tibetan or any other spoken language or dialect; the meanings of each character are traceable, obvious, and little changing with time. Because of this ideographic element, we can get a clearer picture of what the document might mean to us in our own time.

Further, the document in Chinese is a beautiful subject for calligraphy.

What follows is a step by step revisiting of the process I followed in approaching the text as a Westerner and a student of calligraphy. I demanded of myself that I not only had to know how to chant it (in Sino-Japanese) and to copy it, but also to come to an understanding of the text as it was translated into Chinese from Sanskrit and Tibetan originals (again assuming that was the order of events). This required the literal translation of each character, and/or the literal translation rendered by compounds of two or more characters.

Some of the characters and compounds have more than a single literal translation. In such cases I have given all or most of the common meanings, and in cases where questions surround the literal meanings, I have offered notes to comment on them. I felt that if I were to describe my experience, my relationship with the *Shingyō,* I would have to take the reader through this process step by step, which is what I have done here.

John Stevens and Wing-Tsit Chan give us an idea of the enormous task faced by the original translators of the Buddhist canon into Chinese. The sheer volume of documents must have appeared overwhelming. There were four major sects of Buddhism already in place, some still largely influenced by Taoist thought. Committees of scholars and scribes were organized, arguments ensued. One of the most fundamental disagreements surrounded the question of whether any given translation was to be accessible or accurate, poetic or literal. I don't know how that decision came down with regard to the *Shingyō*. I know that in taking on the translation of the *Shingyō* from Chinese into English, we face the same problem.

Translation is an art form requiring an understanding of two cultures, as well as a literal knowledge of both languages (I have little of either, however, I have boldly included three translations of my own). Every translation is an interpretation, and so will reflect the ethos of the culture and era in which it is made, and will also reflect the personal biases and beliefs of the translator, no matter how accurate or neutral the intent. The sutra has been translated many times into English (and other Western languages), in various periods and by translators from diverse religious, philosophical, and scholarly backgrounds. There are many lengthy commentaries, histories, and explanations of it in a great variety of contexts. For example, Conze (1904-1979), who did what was probably the earliest translation, was from the Theosophical movement. Richelt (1877-1952), who did another, was a Protestant Christian missionary in China.

Conze's seems to have set the tone for most of those following. All of them I will refer to, other than those of Mu, Thich, Deshimaru, and the Dalai Lama, largely follow Conze's, and may simply be slight rewordings of it.

In his book, *Taoism: The Parting of the Ways*, Holmes Welch makes clear that Taoism is both a philosophy and a religion, and that over time the two approaches divided, went their separate ways. The same is true of Buddhism, though the split between Philosophical Buddhism and Religious Buddhism may not be so definite. Philosophical Buddhism is sometimes a cosmology (and it is in this aspect that it blurs its differences from the Religious form), but for the most part it is involved with the science of mind. As such, it is sometimes psychological, sometimes epistemological, and sometimes simply instruction in mental self-discipline.

While the vitality of the *Shingyō* is much sustained by the beauty of its calligraphy, is it probably even more alive in the chanting of it. In many cases, the motive for chanting the sutra is solely to gain merit, perhaps as in some Christian contexts the rosary is recited to gain grace. In other cases, it is chanted as a significant aid to *samadhi*, the deep, trance-like state found in meditation. As Stevens explains in some detail, and the Dalai Lama notes, the chanter hears —and somatically experiences— the particular resonances of the string of syllables as (in the former case) magical or (as in the latter) evocative of a state of mind. While the Tibetan version is probably the strongest in this regard, it still carries considerable power to the same effect in Sino-Japanese.

In my opinion, this element is entirely lost when it is chanted in English, although commentary in *The Lotus of the Flame Liturgy* mentions that some of the translations are "not exact or literal . . . in order to render them effective for chanting." I'm afraid this has so far proven a futile effort. The main point of translating it into English seems to me to be to try to form an understanding, first, of what the text actually says; second, what the author might have meant when he wrote it; and only finally, what it might mean to us in our own context. This study is primarily concerned with the first of these purposes.

I am not suggesting that the reader must become familiar with Chinese characters in order to follow the intention of this study. I have done all the dictionary work, and have offered the most neutral translations possible. I'm sure there are more knowledgeable and fluent translators from the Chinese, and I would be grateful if any of them would offer corrections and suggestions for improvements.

Notes on the Illustrations

At the beginning of the book I have shown five versions of the *Shingyō*, copies I have made in my own hand. They are of course not as beautiful as the originals, but are accurate with regard to the original texts. Readers familiar with Chinese characters will note several differences, some of which will be discussed below. Most are simply calligraphic variations, long noted by scholars, which cause no changes in either meaning or pronunciation. Stevens gives a comprehensive list of these on page 124 of his *Sacred Calligraphy of the East*.

The first version is copied from the *Sumidera Shingyō*, the oldest original extant in Japan. Sumidera temple was at the time (Nara Period, 636-794) of the Hōssō sect, derived from the "Consciousness Only" school of Chinese Buddhism (it later changed to the Shingon sect). It is shortened to its essentials, the title reading only "*Shingyō*" and the reprise of the title at the end left out. It uses the simpler version of the character *mu* and for the *i* in *i mu shotoku* (see notes on page 30, below, concerning the *i* in *i mu shotoku*). I find it the most beautifully brushed of all of the originals, although, as noted, the quality of my calligraphy cannot touch this one (or any of them).

The second example is from Myōshinji, the main administrative temple of the Rinzai Zen sect. The writing is in a simpler, more accessible style, and perhaps is relatively modern; it uses the more common forms of the characters for the *sho* in *shotoku* and *kei* in *keigei.*

The third is from Daikakuji, a Shingon temple in the foothills north of Kyoto. One hall there is devoted entirely to the copying of the *Shingyō,* and is open to the public for that purpose. One stops at a kiosk beside the entrance, buys a sheet of paper specifically for sutra copying, a printed copy of the text, and a stick of incense. Inside there is an altar in the ornate Shingon style, and rows of low tables with brushes, inkstones, inksticks, small water containers, and incense burners. One sits in *seiza* at the table, lights one's stick of incense, grinds ink, then copies the sutra. The version copied there is the one shown here. It is in a clear, relatively simple style of block script.

The fourth is that of Harada Rokujisai Kampō. His name "Rokujisai" refers to the mantric phrase in the Jōdō sect of Buddhism (the largest in Japan) suggesting that this was his religious orientation. Even in my poor copy, his bolder version of the clerical style (*shakyō sho*) is evident. It is one of only two I've found that uses the two characters "*butsu setsu*" to begin the title (the other is the one from Daikakuji), and is the only one to use the third variation in the final *shu* noted below.

The last is from Hōsenji. Because it was available only in the printed liturgical pamphlet, and follows the text as I was given it when I attended there, it is in my own handwriting style. It is the only one to use the first variation in the final *shu* on page 51.

A Note to Martial Artists

In the classic tradition of the martial arts in Japan, the brush was considered as important to the samurai as was his sword, bow, or spear. As Dr. Swain put it, "For the true *bushi,* sword and brush become one." Yagyū Munenori, in the *Heihōkadensho,* wrote "*Bun bu ryō dō*", which translates roughly as "Culture and Martial, both Ways." To the Samurai, as was true even earlier in Taoist and Confucian China, a fine hand with the brush denoted the cultured man. My teacher of swordsmanship, Morikawa Gembu, was a serious calligrapher, following the examples of Kagawa Zenjirō and Yamaoka Tesshu, all of the Mutō-ryu school of Kendō.

This text was one commonly written by warriors. It may well have much to say to both Chinese and Japanese martial artists about the state of the mind in martial practice, especially to those in the internal styles.

And a Final Reminder

Again (and again and again): Every translation is an interpretation, and so will reflect the ethos of the culture and era in which it is made, and will also reflect the personal biases and beliefs of the translator, no matter how accurate or neutral the intent.

Shingyō:

The text, with romanized Sino-Japanese pronunciations
(The Hepburn System is used throughout),
Approximate Literal Meanings in English,
Notes and Comments

The Lotus in the Flame Temple Liturgy states (on page 47) that "the text of the . . . *Maka Hannya Haramita Shin Gyō* . . . (is) a Sanskrit transliteration into Sino-Japanese." This is not strictly the case. Several of the words and phrases are indeed just phonetic renderings of the Sanskrit, but the text as a whole is not. Those that are Sanskrit phonetic renderings:

Maka;
Hannya Haramita;
Bosatsu;
Bo-dai-(or -ji-) -satsu;
Sharishi;
Nehan;
San-myaku-san-bo-dai,
and the closing mantra.
These will be shown in negative.

Dictionaries:

Chen, Janey: *A Practical English-Chinese Pronouncing Dictionary.* Tuttle, 1970.

Goodrich, Chauncey: *Chinese-English Pocket Dictionary.* Hong Kong University Press, 1965.

Kaifeng: *A Modern Chinese-English Dictionary.* Oxford University Press, 1960.

Kawamoto, et al: *The Kodansha English-Japanese Dictionary.* Kodansha, 1969

Nelson, Andrew N.: *The Modern Reader's Japanese-English Character Dictionary* (second revised edition). Tuttle,1984.

Takahashi Morio: *Romanized English-Japanese Japanese-English Dictionary.* Taiseido, 1953.

Of these, the Nelson has been the most consistently useful. While the usage of Chinese characters in China has changed radically over the generations, the Japanese usage has remained largely the same since the 6th century. The "Chinese Glossary" in Chan's *A Sourcebook in Chinese Philosophy* was also often of immense help.

Note 1. As part of the title, these two characters are used simply to render the Sanskrit sounds, *maha*. Here, as in all such cases following, it is of much interest to note the meanings of the characters chosen to represent the sounds.

Note 2. The same is true of the next six characters in the title. These render the Sanskrit "*Prajna Paramita*". This is usually translated as "Highest Wisdom", but the way it is frequently used in this text suggests that here it may mean "meditation". This is to some degree a matter of sectarian interpretation.

Note 3. *shin*: Does "Heart" properly translate "*hridaya*" as it was meant or understood in Sanskrit? Does "Heart" properly translate the Chinese character "*shin*"? For that matter, did "*shin*" properly translate the word from Sanskrit to Chinese in the first place? I have often encountered this character translated into English as "heart/mind" in the Japanese tradition, and, recently, found "heart/mind" as the translation of the related Thai term. Both Goodrich[1] and W. T. Chan[2] translate the Chinese "*shin*" as "mind" rather than "heart". All this seems to me to be evidence that the distinction we draw between heart and mind is not the same one drawn in these Buddhist and pre-Buddhist cultures, if they in fact draw any distinction between the two concepts at all. Mu[3] deals with this question briefly, but very well, in the first paragraph of his Introduction; however, he moves away from it quickly and does not address it specifically again.

This character is used twice more in the document. It occurs in the phrase usually translated into English as, "no obstructions, therefore, mind having no fear", and at the very end, "*Hannya Shingyō*" (which can be taken as an abbreviated reprise of the title). In any case, it is usually translated as "mind" in the phrase in the main text, and as "heart" in the title and the reprise. This seems to indicate that, while the Chinese considered the character to have one meaning in both contexts, the translators into English have needed two words for it (Dr. Shan wrote to me to say, "You are right that this character has one meaning in both contexts.").

[1]Goodrich, Chauncey: *Chinese-English Pocket Dictionary.* Hong Kong University Press, 1965.

[2]Chan Wing-Tsit: *A Source Book in Chinese Philosophy.* Princeton University Press, 1963.

[3]Mu Soeng Sunim: *Heart Sutra: Ancient Buddhist Wisdom in the Light of Quantum Reality.* Primary Point Press, 1991.

ma	} Note 1.	to polish
ka		to proclaim
han	Note 2.	carry
nya		young
ha		wave
ra		silk gauze
mi		honey; nectar
ta		many
shin	Note 3.	
gyō		classic or sacred text

Note 4. *Kan-ji-zai:*The translation of this name of the Buddhist deity Avalokitesvara from Sanskrit into Chinese raises an interesting question: Why didn't the translators render "Avalokitesvara" phonetically, as they did "Maja Prajna Parimita", "Shariputra", "Nirvana", "Anuttara Samyak Sambodhi", *etc*.? Wing-tsit Chan says that Avalokitesvara was instantly identified by the Chinese with Kuan-yin, the god (and subsequently, goddess) of mercy. Even so, it is then still curious why they did not use the usual characters for Kuan-yin, (観 音 Japanese *Kan-0n*, "Contemplates the Sound") or Kan-ze-on, (観 世 音 "Contemplates the World's Sound") but used rather the *Kan-ji-zai* characters, which mean "Contemplates the Self's Region", "Contemplates Freely", or "Contemplates Freedom" (See "A Final and Fanciful Note on the Authorship of Shingyō," where the Wade-Giles Romanization in Chinese, Kuan-Tzu-Ts'ai for Kan-ji-sai is used).

Note 5. *bosatsu:* The shortest, usually titular, way of phonetically rendering the Sanskrit *Bodhisattva*. (Another form of this will appear later in the text: *bodaisatsuta*). In the Mahayana tradition, a Bodhisattva is a kind of saint, generally seen as one who attains Enlightenment, but refuses Nirvana in order to remain in the world to "save all living beings". There are some sectarian variations to this view, and it is not held in the Pali tradition.

(A General note here: written Classical Chinese has no inherent distinctions between singular and plural, and none regarding verb tenses or conjugations. These distinctions require specific additional characters, in the absence of which any given phrase or sentence can be in any tense, case, form or number.)

観	*kan*	contemplate	
自	*ji*	self	} Note 4
在	*zai*	location; presence; existence	
菩	*bo-*	a kind of grass or tree	} Note 5
薩	*satsu*	Buddha	
行	*gyō*	going; doing; action	
深	*shin*	deep	
般	*han-*	carry	(See Note 2, above)
若	*-ya-*	young	
波	*-ha-*	wave	
羅	*-ra-*	silk gauze	
蜜	*-mi-*	honey; nectar	
多	*-ta*	many	
時	*ji*	time	

Note 6. *go-un:* Renders the five *skandhas*. It literally means "five accumulations, piles, or stacks" (the Dalai Lama gives us "aggregates"; Hoffman, "conditions"; Boeree, "aspects of human existence"; while the rest leave *skandhas* un-translated). Many religions like to establish set numbers of concepts in categories (the Seven Deadly Sins, the Five Confucian virtues, the Four Noble Truths, etc. See "the Three Worlds", below). My best guess here is that the five *skandhas* are meant to be categories of remembered experiences, but there are several possible variations. I feel sure that "the five senses" is not one of them.

Note 7. *Sharishi*: This is the Sino-Japanese rendering of the name of the Buddha's best disciple, Shariputra. The "Sha-ri" is definitely phonetic, but the "shi" may be an honorific for classical teachers and authors (e.g. Rō-shi [老子, Lao-tze], Kō-shi [孔子, Confucius], etc.). It is used twice in the text, as a way to set the scene in which Kanjizai lectures Sharishi. The body of the text is usually considered as the content of that lecture.

照	*shō*	clear(ly)
見	*ken*	to see
五	*go*	five
	} Note 6	
蘊	*un*	pile(s); accumulations
皆	*kai*	all
空	*kū*	sky; space; emptiness
度	*do*	save; salvation
一	*i*	(one)
	}	all; every
切	*sai*	(cut)
苦	*ku*	suffering
厄	*yaku*	misfortune
舍	*sha-*	inn; mansion
利	*-ri-*} (see Note 7.)	benefit; profit
子	*-shi*	child; prince

This is probably the most frequently quoted phrase from the text, and probably the most difficult. To start with, all the translators I've found give "form" for *shiki* (except Boeree, who gives us "body"). While *shiki* (using this character) has indeed several meanings, in all my dictionaries they fall in one way or another under the categories I've offered here. There are two or three characters which mean "form" quite clearly, in many or all contexts (e.g. 形 , 型). Further, later, as will be noted, the character *shiki* is used in other contexts, where the translation is not "form", but "color" or, in one case, "objects of sight" (the San Francisco translation sticks to "form" at that point).

On the other hand, *kū* is almost always given in English as "emptiness," or sometimes as "void," "sky," or "space". Mu, in his interpretive commentary, expands on "emptiness" at great length, making it clear that he considers it vital and essential to an understanding of the text as a whole.

色	*shiki*	color; sensuality
不	*fu*	not
異	*i*	different
空	*kū*	sky; space; emptiness; void
空	*kū*	"
不	*fu*	not
異	*i*	different
色	*shiki*	color; sensuality
色	*shiki*	"
即	*soku*	exact(ly)
是	*ze*	this; thus
空	*kū*	sky; space; emptiness; void
空	*kū*	"
即	*soku*	exact(ly)
是	*ze*	this; thus
色	*shiki*	color; sensuality

The group into a phrase of *"ju / sō / gyō / shiki"* appears again in the text. While the preceding phrase, *shiki fu i kū,* refers to the first of the five *skandhas,* these are the other four. The phrase appears again on page 23, following *mu shiki,* thus referring again to the five *skandhas*. This phrase seems to me to end the introductory paragraph.

"Sharishi" is, in all the translations I've seen, used as the beginning of the two sentences in which it appears, and is probably traditionally so in Sanskrit and Tibetan. However, as the classical Chinese version has no punctuation, and if one confines oneself to the Chinese, it could as well be placed at the ends of the preceding ones. I have found this approach more convenient in breaking the phrases down for memorization, chanting and calligraphy. Further, it seems especially appropriate in regard to the *shiki fu i kū* sequence, which, when quoted separately, almost always starts with *shiki fu i kū,* not *Sharishi, shiki fu i kū*.

As a translator into modern English, I would probably end the second paragraph with this line. Up to this point, the text seems intended to be read as both an epistemological and a cosmological description. The sutra as a whole can, and has been, interpreted as exclusively either, or as both at once (see note on this subject in "The Hermit and the *Shingyō*" on page 59 below).

ju	receiving
sō	imagining
gyō	going; doing
shiki	knowing
yaku	also
bu	return; revert
nyō	like
ze	this
sha-	inn; mansion
ri-} (see Note 7.)	benefit; profit
shi	child; prince

Note 8. *hō*: In other than Buddhist contexts, this is usually translated as "Rules, methods, laws, etc." In the Buddhist context, it is a rendering of "Dharma". A solid definition of "Dharma" appears to be complicated. The Dalai Lama gives "phenomena" in this first phrase, and "mental objects" in a later one. Dr. C.W. Swain suggests that "teachings" might be accurate. Another alternative might be "received wisdom." W.T. Chan gives us "that which is held to." Perhaps, then, in this context, it may mean "doctrine", "dogma" or "belief." (Dr. Swain insists that it does not mean "belief." I'm not certain if our definitions of the word "belief" agree. I define "belief" as a proposition, statement, or assumption, which cannot be verified or falsified, proved or disproved, yet is considered to be true. Note also that, of the cited translations, three leave the word "Dharma" un-translated, and one skips this phrase entirely (this character appears again, in the phrase on page 25).

Note 9. *sō*: This character *sō* (相) also has several meanings, which clearly change as contexts change. However, it often implies "similar to," "corresponding to" or "reciprocal." It is composed of two elements, "wood" or "tree" on the left, "eye" on the right. The "wood" element often implies "real," "actual," "material" (as opposed to "imaginary"). When the *shin* element is added to 相, as in *ju sō* (想) *gyō shiki* and, later, in *musō* (夢想 "dream, vision, reverie"), the meaning becomes "imagined," "mental," or some other concept having to do with mind.

ze	this; thus
sho	all
hō	Note 8.
kū	sky; space; emptiness
sō	Note 9.

不	*fu*	without; not
生	*shō*	birth; beginning
不	*fu*	without; not
滅	*metsu*	end; extinction
不	*fu*	without; not
垢	*ku*	taint; impurities
不	*fu*	without; not
浄	*jō*	purity; clarity
不	*fu*	without; not
増	*sō*	increase
不	*fu*	without; not
減	*gen*	decrease

ze	this; thus
ko	therefore
kū	emptiness, sky
chū	center; middle of
mu	without; not; no
shiki	color; sensuality
mu	without; not; no
ju	(note that this *ju*, and the three characters following, stand as a group and are translated on page 19, above)
sō	
gyō	
shiki	

Starting with *"ze ko kū chū,"* (Therefore/within/emptiness) this paragraph seems to me to intend to describe the condition of the mind during deep meditation, and so drops any cosmological implication to become entirely psychological or epistemological.

Again, the character *hō* for *dharma* appears, following a list which is sometimes referred to as the "inner *shiki*" (色), after the list of the "outer *shiki*", plus *i* (in all but one case, translated as "mind" or "thought"). So here, in the same way that "No eye, ear," etc. are balanced by "no color, sound," etc., *hō* balances *i*, and seems to mean any thoughts or, as the Dalai Lama puts it in this instance, "mental objects."

無	*mu*	no
眼	*gen*	eyes
耳	*ni*	ears
鼻	*bi*	nose
舌	*setsu*	tongue
身	*shin*	body
意	*i*	thought; idea; intention
無	*mu*	no
色	*shiki*	color
聲	*shō*	sound
香	*kō*	scent
味	*mi*	taste; flavor
觸	*soku*	touch; texture
法	*hō*	(see Note 8)

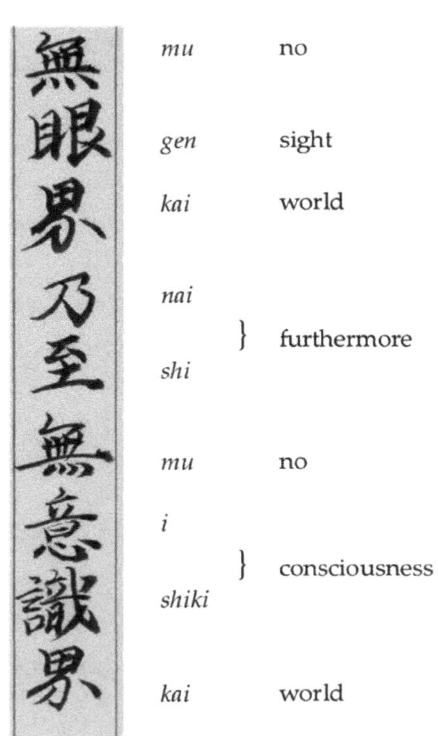
無眼界乃至無意識界
mu no
gen sight
kai world
nai
} furthermore
shi
mu no
i
} consciousness
shiki
kai world

無	*mu*	no
無明	*mu myō*	ignorance
亦	*yaku*	also
無	*mu*	no
無明	*mu myō*	ignorance
盡	*jin*	exhaustion
乃至	*nai shi*	furthermore
無	*mu*	no
老	*rō*	old age
死	*shi*	death
亦	*yaku*	also
無	*mu*	no
老	*rō*	old age
死	*shi*	death
盡	*jin*	exhaustion

Note 10. *dō*: This character has many meanings, largely determined by context. As *Tao*, in China, an entire philosophy is derived from it (Taoism), as is a religion of the same name (The philosophy and the religion, though related, are not the same. See Holmes Welch[4] for details as to the development of Taoism). W. T. Chan offers seventeen different commentaries on the character, from different periods, different philosophies and religions, and different thinkers from each of those philosophies and religions. The Nelson *Japanese-English Dictionary*[5] lists twenty-three different meanings in English. It becomes, then, a matter of deciding what it means in any particular context.

I have offered "Path" as a simple, literal English meaning. This is clearly inadequate. The range of meanings is on a scale from the entirely mundane ("road, highway, path," etc.) to the extreme of transcendence ("The Way that can be named is not the Way", Lao-tzu says in the first statement of the *Tao Te Ching*). Considering the times in which this was translated from Sanskrit to Chinese, it seems possible that here the "absence of the path" is meant to reject the Taoism of Lao-tzu and later Taoists. On the other hand, the word is in a grouping with "suffering, collecting and extinction", suggesting that it has more to do with ordinary human experience, but may refer specifically to the Buddhist "Eight-Fold Path." Later, in Buddhist Japan, the character came to refer to arts and occupations (way of tea, way of calligraphy, way of swordsmanship, etc.), all of which seemed to imply disciplined routes toward Buddhist enlightenment.

Note 11. *toku*: The text says here, quite clearly, "No attainment (profit; benefit)". This character is used twice more in the text. Later it will say that all Buddhas "*attain* Perfect Enlightenment", which seems to me to be something of a contradiction.

[4]Welch, Holmes: Taoism: *The Parting of the Way*. Beacon Press, 1957, 1965.

[5]Nelson, Andrew N.: *The Modern Reader's Japanese-English Character Dictionary*. Tuttle, 1984.

無	*mu*	no
苦	*ku*	suffering
集	*shu*	collecting
滅	*metsu*	extinction
道	*dō* Note 10.	path
無	*mu*	no
智	*chi*	knowledge; wisdom
亦	*yaku*	also
無	*mu*	no
得	*toku* Note 11.	attainment; profit; advantage

Note 12. I would as a translator start a new paragraph with this phrase, *i-mu-sho-toku*. The Dalai Lama[6], translating from Tibetan, does so:

"Therefore . . . since bodhisattvas have no attainments . . . . "

As does the translation from Stevens[7]:

"Indeed, there is nothing to be attained.. . . ."

And that of Thich[8]:

"Because there is no attainment. . . ."

Mu does not, but rather uses the equivalent phrase to end the previous paragraph with, "there being nothing to attain." Boeree takes the same approach, ending the previous paragraph with, "and no wisdom to attain."

Hoffman, having rendered the sutra in verse, has no paragraphs as such, but gives as a separate line:

"With nothing to attain. . . ."

The Chinese approach here is slightly different. *Shotoku* (a compound using the "*toku*" of Note 11), according to all my dictionaries, Chinese-English, English-Chinese, English-Japanese and Japanese-English, means "earnings", "livelihood" or "possessions". For the educated Chinese of the time, it probably also meant "employment" or "position", as a place in the bureaucracy was the only key to success. The phrase in Chinese might be translated as:

"Because (or *"to use"* or *"in view of"*; the Sumidera version uses a different *i* [已] which can mean "Already") */ no / earnings (or livelihood or possessions). . .*

It appears that none of translations into English published so far address this Chinese view of the sentence. All translations are necessarily interpretations, granted, but this strikes me as going rather farther than just interpretation. I can account for it only by assuming that the translators have found unacceptable the idea that the bodhisattva must not work for a living, must renounce the material life, and must live in poverty.

[6]The Dalai Lama: *Essence of the Heart Sutra.* Wisdom Publications, 2005.

[7]Stevens, John: *Sacred Calligraphy of the East.* Shambhala, 1981.

[8]Thich Nhat Hanh: *The Heart of Understanding.* Parallax Press, 1988, 2009.

i		to use; because; in view of
mu		no
sho	} Note 12.	possessions; earnings; employment
toku		

Note 13. As mentioned in Note 5, *bodaisastuta*, or *bodhisattva*, is one who has reached Buddhist Enlightenment, but stays in the world to save all living things, and in this way is different from a Buddha, who goes on to Nirvana. Notice that in this text, however, the *bodhisattva* reaches Nirvana, while later, the (three) Buddha(s) (佛) attain(s) "Highest and most Perfect Enlightenment." The Dalai Lama's commentary suggests that there is no difference (p 127ff).

ko	therefore
bo	a kind of grass
dai	carry
} Note 13.	
satsu	Buddha
ta	close; plug up
e	rely on
(see Note 2. for this and the next five characters)	

故	*ko*	therefore
心	*shin*	heart/mind
無	*mu*	without
罣	*kei*	} obstruction
礙	*gei*	
無	*mu*	without
罣	*kei*	} obstruction
礙	*gei*	
故	*ko*	therefore
無	*mu*	without
有	*u*	have
恐	*ku*	} fear
怖	*fu*	

遠	*on-*	far (from)
離	*ri*	
一	*i-*	all
切	*sai*	
顛	*ten-*	tumbling; falling down; tipping over
倒	*tō*	
夢	*mu-*	dreams, fantasies
想	*sō*	
究	*kū-*	finally
竟	*kyō*	
涅	*ne-*	black soil (phonetic: *Nirvana)*
槃	*han*	tub

Note 14: "Three Worlds": Some translations call the three worlds those of "Past, Present, and Future". The Dalai Lama says "the three times." Some simply skip the phrase. W. T. Chan gives us the three worlds as those of "Desire, Matter, and Pure Spirit" (also see Note 6. on the five *skandhas,* above).

san	} Note 14.	three
zei		worlds
sho		all
butsu		Buddha(s)
e		rely on
(see Note 2. for this and the next five characters)		

Note 15: *A-noku-ta-ra-san-myaku-sambodai*: This is the phonetic rendering of the Sanskrit "Anuttara Samyak Sambodhi". The San Francisco Zen Center translation gives us "the most supreme enlightenment." Mu and Hoffman leave it un-translated. Thich says "full, right, and universal Enlightenment"; Boeree and the Lotus in the Flame, "full enlightenment" (also see note on page 32).

ko		therefore
toku		attain (see Note 10.)
a	(next 8 characters phonetics only)	Note 15.
noku		
ta		
ra		
san		
myaku		
san		
bo		
dai		

Note 16: Some commentaries have suggested that the essence of the sutra, from a philosophical point of view, ends here, and that from the phrase, *ze / dai / jin / shu*, the rest preceding the actual mantra is mainly an exhortation to recite it.

ko therefore

chi know

(see Note 2. for this and the next five characters)

(see Note 16)

Note 17. *shu*: Sanskrit *dharani* (some translations), or *mantra*. That is to say, all of the translations have left the word un-translated. The dictionaries give us Spell, Curse, or Incantation. In this context, I think we can assume it to refer to a sound, word, or phrase intoned to help open the mind to Hannya Haramita. Other examples of *shu* are *Om Mani Padme Hūm* from Tibet, and *Namu Amida Butsu* from the Jōdō Buddhist sect in Japan. Of such, the single syllables *Om, Aom*, and *Mu* are probably the most common.

是大神咒是大明咒			
	ze		this
	dai		great
	jin		sacred
	shu	Note 17.	incantation
	ze		this
	dai		great
	myō		bright; clear
	shu	Note 17.	incantation

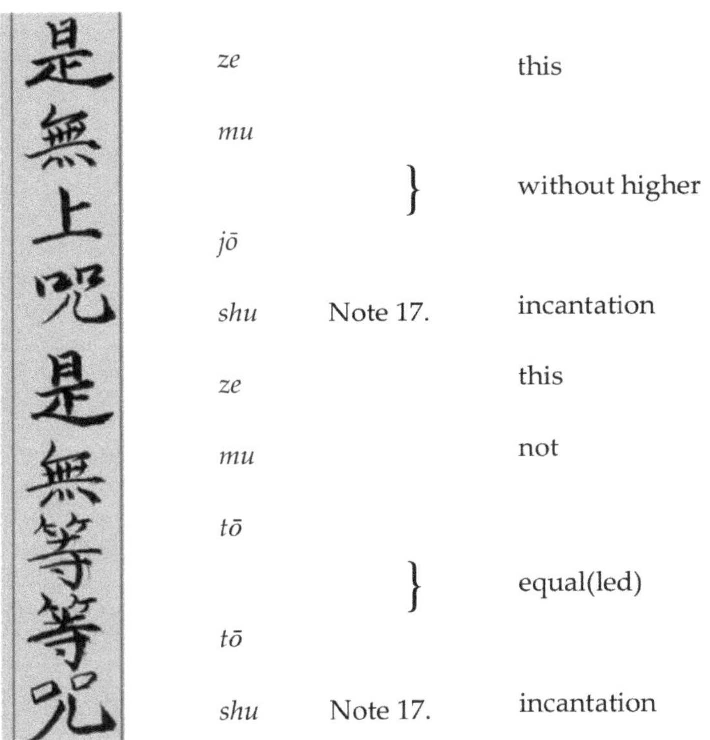

是	*ze*		this
無	*mu*	}	without higher
上	*jō*		
呪	*shu*	Note 17.	incantation
是	*ze*		this
無	*mu*		not
等	*tō*	}	equal(led)
等	*tō*		
呪	*shu*	Note 17.	incantation

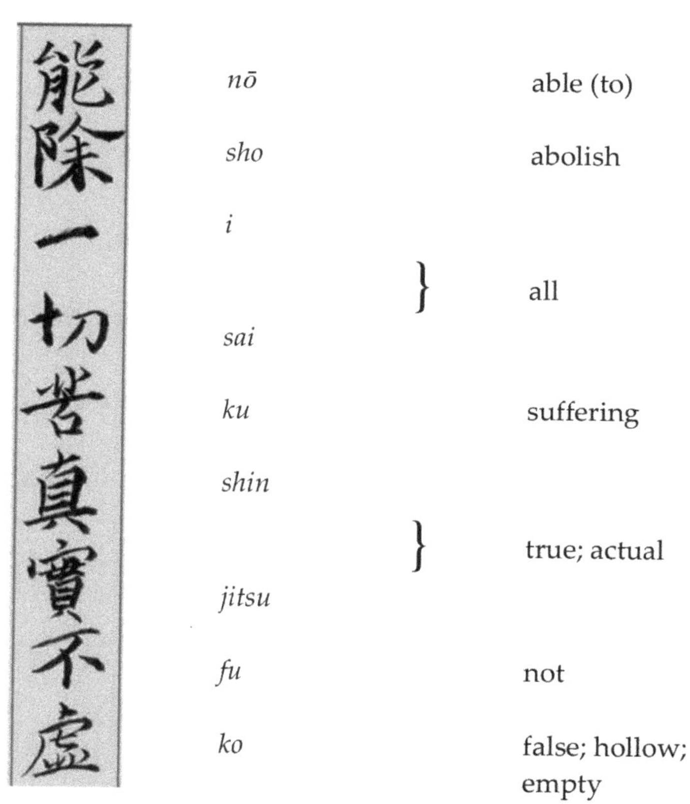

能除一切苦真實不虛

能	*nō*	able (to)
除	*sho*	abolish
一	*i*	all
切	*sai*	
苦	*ku*	suffering
真	*shin*	true; actual
實	*jitsu*	
不	*fu*	not
虛	*ko*	false; hollow; empty

故	*ko*	therefore
説	*setsu*	recite; intone
般若波羅蜜多	(see Note 2. for this and the next five characters)	
呪	*shu*	incantation
即	*soku*	exact(ly)
説	*setsu*	recite; intone
呪	*shu*	incantation
曰	*watsu*	saying

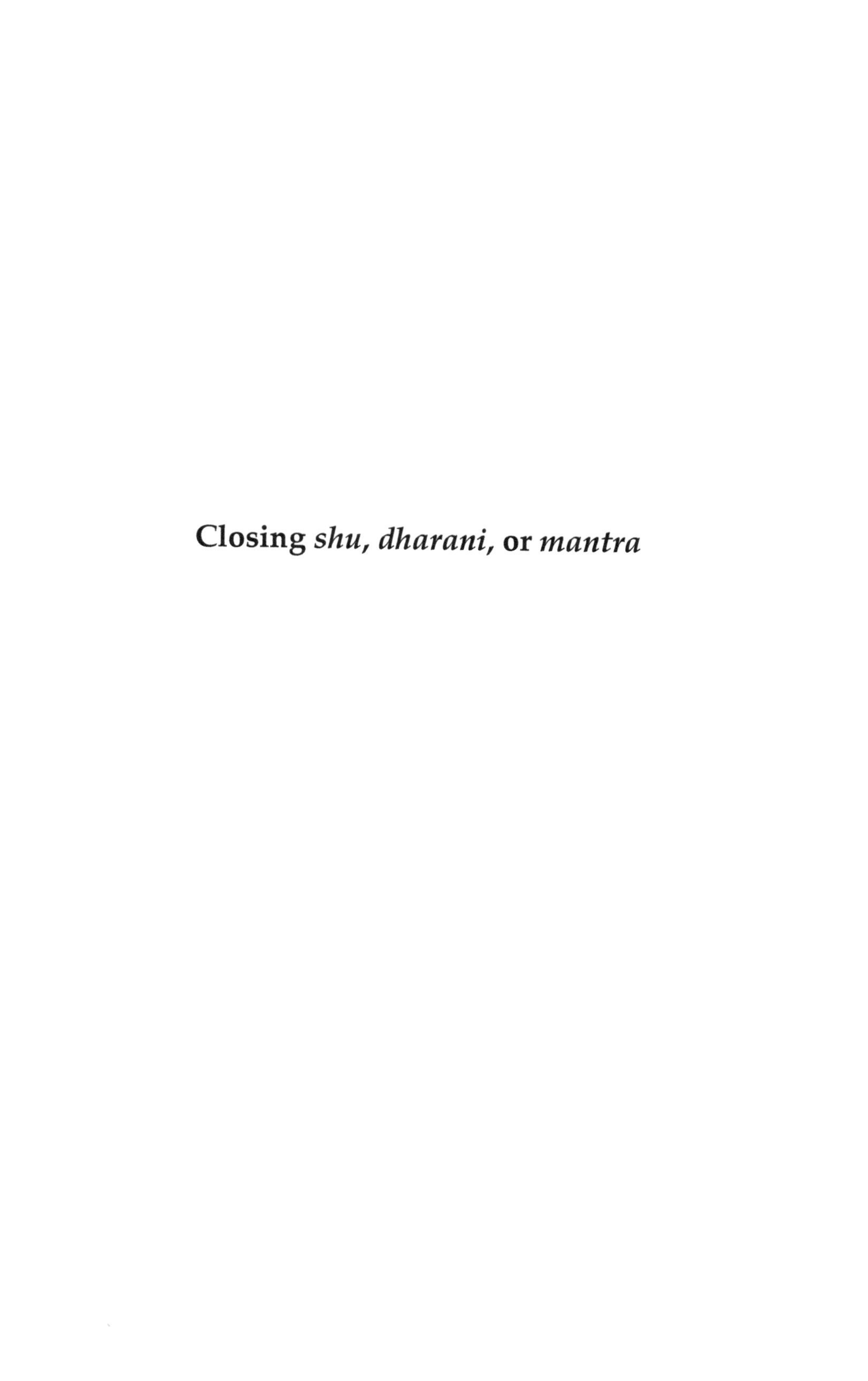

Closing *shu, dharani,* or *mantra*

Note 18: This is the *shu* which I recall, roughly, Allen Ginsberg as having translated as "Beyond, beyond, even beyond Beyond, the priest has gone." This is perhaps somewhat more poetic than literal. Of all the translations and commentaries I've consulted, only three translate this *shu*: The Dalai Lama (in the commentary, not the translation), Thich, and Boeree (both of whom do so only after the Sanskrit phonetic rendering). This is, I think, because all recognize the importance of the effect the sounds of the syllables have on the state of the mind in meditation (see my note on page 3, last paragraph, above).

羯	*gya-*		beyond
諦	*te*		
羯	*gya-*		beyond
諦	*te*		
波	*ha-*	wave	ultimate
羅	*ra*	silk gauze	
羯	*gya-*		beyond
諦	*te*		
波	*ha-*	wave	ultimate
羅	*ra*	silk gauze	
僧	*sō*	priest; monk	
羯	*gya-*		beyond
諦	*te*		

Note 19. *bo-ji*: The Sino-Japanese phonetic rendering of the Sanskrit *bodhi*. This is usually translated as "wisdom," "awakened," or "enlightenment."

sowa; sowaka:

The Sino-Japanese phonetic rendering of the Sanskrit *svaha*. Some translations give us "Hurrah!". Some translations, "So be it!" The characters used in Variation One for this are those taken from the Hōsenji print version, and both mean literally "old woman". Together in a compound they refer to "this corrupt world" and are in other contexts pronounced *shaba*. Those in Variation Two are the previously noted *satsu* (for Buddha) and *ba* (for "old woman"). These seem to be the most common, used in the Sumidera, Daikakuji, and Myōshinji. Those in Variation Three are, first, the same *satsu*, and then, the *ha* meaning "wave". This is from this Kampō version (in some others he used those in Variation Two).

None of these account for the following *ka*. For this *ka*, the dictionaries give us Scold, Blame, or Reprove. It may be that it is used here simply as a vocalized exclamation point. I think, though, that when the *shaba* characters are used, as in the Hōsenji version, it might be translated as "Reproving this corrupt world".

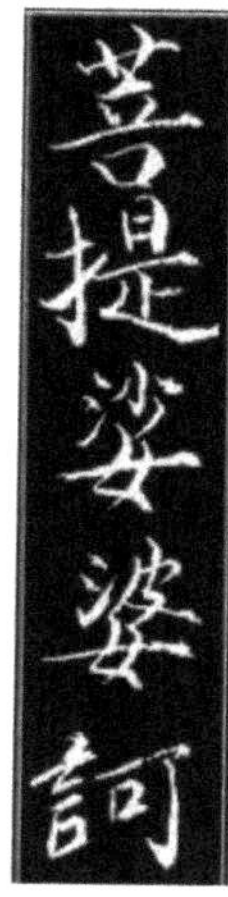

菩 *bo-* } wisdom Note 19.
提 *ji*

(variation one)

娑 *so-* } Skt. *svaha.*
婆 *wa*
訶 *ka* spell; curse; incantation

(variation two)

薩 *so-* } Skt. *svaha*
婆 *wa*
呵 *ka* spell; curse; incantation

(variation three)

薩 *so-* } Skt. *svaha.*
波 *wa*
呵 *ka* spell; curse; incantation

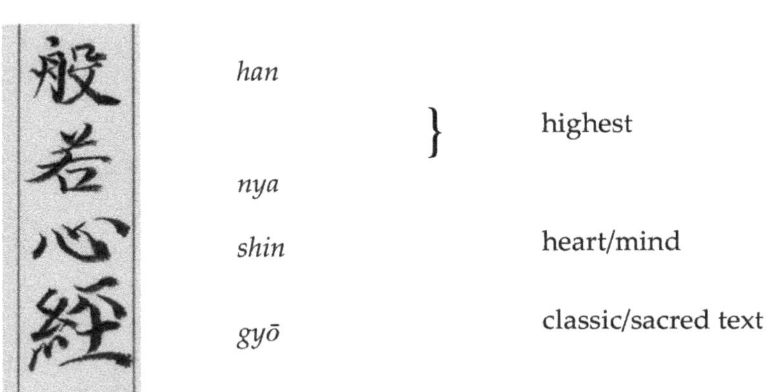

Abbreviated
Reprise of the
Title

MAHA PRAJNA PARAMITA HEART SUTRA

Avalokiteshvara Bodhisattva, practicing deep Prajna Paramita
Clearly saw that all five conditions are empty,
Thus was relieved from all suffering and fear.
O Shariputra, form is no other than emptiness,
emptiness no other than form.
Form is exactly emptiness, emptiness exactly form.
Sensation, perception, discrimination, awareness
are likewise like this.
O Shariputra, all dharmas are forms of emptiness;
Not born, not destroyed, not tainted, not pure,
without gain, without loss.
So, in emptiness there is no form, no sensation,
perception, discrimination, awareness;
No eye, ear, nose, tongue, body, mind;
No color, sound, smell, taste, touch, phenomena;
No realm of sight, and so forth until no realm of consciousness;
No ignorance, and no extinction of it, and so forth until
no old age and death and extinction of them;
No suffering, no cause of suffering, no extinguishing,
no path, no wisdom and no gain.
With nothing to attain, the Bodhisattva lives Prajna Paramita.
With no hindrance in the mind, there is no hindrance,
therefore no fear exists.
Far beyond deluded thoughts, this is Nirvana.
All past, present and future Buddhas live Prajna Paramita
And therefore attain Anuttara Samyak Sambodhi!
Therefore know, Prajna Paramita is the great mantra
Is the great bright mantra
is the supreme mantra
is the unsurpassable mantra.
It is capable of relieving all suffering,
This is true, not false.
So proclaim the Prajna Paramita Mantra.
Proclaim this mantra and say:
Gate! Gate! Paragate! Parasamgate! Bodhi! Svaha!

Version in English by Djann Hoffman
from the San Francisco Zen Center translation

Following are, first, a translation largely following the traditional one from the San Francisco Zen Center, with notes on un-translated terms. There are some variations and perhaps expansions.

Second, a translation in which I have inserted my own translations of all the un-translated terms. These will surely invite some argument.

Third, a translation which reflects the "Radical Zen" view (Robert Bellah's term in his book, *Tokugawa Religion*), as suggested in the phrase "Rejecting all supernatural elements." This version also eliminates the references to mythic-legendary characters, and removes all narrative form. Some explanations for decisions made in this version follow it.

A Translation of The Heart Sutra, with Notes

Hannya Haramita Shingyõ

Kanjizai-bosatsu, when in deep meditation, clearly saw that the Go-un are empty, and so was saved from all suffering and misfortune, Sharishi.

"Colors are not different from emptiness, emptiness is not different from colors. Colors are exactly emptiness, emptiness is exactly color. The same is true of feelings, thoughts, impulses, and consciousness, Sharishi.

"All dharmas are empty expressions. They do not appear or disappear, are not tainted or pure, do not increase or decrease. Therefore, in emptiness, no eyes, no ears, no nose, no tongue, no body, no mind; no color, no sound, no smell, no taste, no touch, no object of mind, no realm of eyes and so forth until no realm of mind and consciousness. No ignorance and also no extinction of ignorance and so forth until no old age and death and also no extinction of old age and death.

"No suffering, no craving, no extinction, no path; no wisdom, no accomplishment.

"Having no possessions, the Bojisatsu depends on meditation and the heart/mind is un-obstructed. Having no obstructions, he has no fears. Far beyond dreams and imaginings, at last Nirvana. In the San Ze, each Buddha depends on meditation and attains the highest enlightenment. Therefore know Hannya haramita.

"This great sacred mantra, the great bright mantra, the utmost mantra, the supreme mantra, is able to relieve all suffering. It is true and not false. So proclaim the Hannya Haramita mantra, proclaim this mantra and say:

"Gyate, gyate, hara gyate, hara so gyate, Bojisō waka.

"Hannya Shingyō."

Un-translated terms:

Sutra: Literally, a thread. A classic document, usually, as in this case, sacred.

Hannya haramita: The Japanese rendering of Prajna Paramita. "Prajna" means "wisdom." "Paramita" means "highest." This also means, in this text especially, the practice of meditation, particularly the state of *zanmai,* 三昧 the Japanese rendering of the Sanskrit *samadhi.*

Shingyō : The Heart Sutra, classic, or thread. *Shin* is as often translated as "mind," but in Chinese or Japanese (and perhaps other Asian languages) is not distinguished from "heart," and so is often translated as "heart/mind").

Kanjisai-bosatsu: This refers to the archetype of compassion, Kannon, Kuan-Yin, or Avalokitesvara (in Japanese, Chinese, and Sanskrit respectively). It is not clear why here the figure is not "Kuan-Yin," but "Kanjisai," literally "Contemplate Self's Existence" or "Contemplate Freedom."

Go-un: The five *skandhas* in Sanskrit (literally "five piles or stacks"). These are colors (the visible world, or in some cases, sensuality), sensation, perception, mental formations, and consciousness, and are considered the essential elements of personality.

Sharishi: This refers to the best disciple of the Buddha, Shariputra.

San Ze: The Three Worlds, perhaps of desire, matter, and pure spirit (see below).

Bojisatsuta: Bodhisattva, an enlightened one who refuses to complete his attainment of Nirvana in order to live to save all living beings. In the Mahayana tradition, the highest spiritual attainment.

Mantra (*shu* in Japanese): A syllable, word, or phrase chanted or imagined as an aid to meditation.

Gyate, gyate, hara gyate, hara so gyate, Bo ji sō wa ka Hannya Shingyō: "Beyond, beyond, even beyond Beyond, goeth the priest (This is a rendering from the Sanskrit. Translation by Allen Ginsberg.).

"Hannya Shingyō." The Highest Heart/Mind Sutra.

A Translation of The Heart Sutra, with no un-translated words

The Classic of the Highest Wisdom Heart/Mind

The Goddess of Mercy, when going deeply into the highest wisdom, clearly saw that the Five Stacks are empty, and so was saved from all suffering and misfortune, 0 Best Student.

"Colors are not different from emptiness, emptiness is not different from colors. Colors are exactly emptiness, emptiness is exactly color. The same is true of feelings, thoughts, impulses, and consciousness, 0 Best Student.

"All doctrines are empty expressions. They do not appear or disappear, are not tainted or pure, do not increase or decrease. Therefore, in emptiness, no eyes, no ears, no nose, no tongue, no body, no mind; no color, no sound, no smell, no taste, no touch, no object of mind, no realm of sight and so forth until no realm of imagination or thought. No ignorance and also no extinction of ignorance and so depends on highest wisdom and the mind and so forth until no old age and death and also no extinction of old age and death.

"No suffering, no craving, no extinction, no path; no wisdom, no attainment.

"Having no possessions, the Enlightened One has no hindrance. Without hindrance, no fears exist. Far beyond perverted views at last peaceful joy. In the three worlds, each Enlightened One depends on highest wisdom and attains the highest enlightenment. Therefore know highest wisdom.

"This great transcendent incantation, the great bright incantation, the utmost incantation, the supreme incantation, is able to relieve all suffering. It is true and not false. So proclaim the highest wisdom incantation, proclaim this incantation and say:

"Beyond, beyond, even beyond Beyond, goeth the priest."

A "Radical Zen" Version

The Sacred Classic of the Mind/Spirit

A wise person, contemplating the self's existence, goes deeply into the meditative state and sees clearly that the five kinds of accumulations of experiences which have shaped the mind are all empty. Seeing this relieves all suffering and misfortune.

The accumulations of sensory experiences are not different from emptiness (and vice versa). The accumulations of sensory experiences are exactly the same as emptiness (and vice versa). Indoctrinations, imaginings, training (as in muscle memory), and thoughts are just like this.

So, all our rules are empty expressions, without birth or ending, without impurity or purity, increase or decrease.

In the midst of emptiness there are no indoctrinations, imaginings, training (as in muscle memory), or thoughts. No eyes, ears, nose, tongue, body or mind. No objects of sight, sound, scent, taste, touch, or thought. No seen world, also no world of the mind/spirit. No ignorance and no end to ignorance. No old age and death and no end to old age and death. No suffering, collecting, endings, or path. No wisdom, no accomplishment.

Having no possessions, the wise one relies on the meditative state, and so has the mind/spirit without obstructions. No obstructions, therefore no fear. Far beyond all falling into dreams and imaginings, at last, peace of mind.

All wise ones in each of the three worlds rely on the meditative state and so attain the most perfect wisdom. Therefore, come to know the meditative state.

Notes:

The accurate translation of *ku-yaku* would probably be "misfortune," which I have used here. Hoffman used "fear," Levine used "misfortune and suffering." Others have used "pain." (Also see *shotoku* below.)

I have read some commentaries stating that Zen has evolved from an intuitive practice into an intellectual philosophy. I think there may be some truth in the idea, as I have read a number of books on the subject, have listened to many "Dharma Talks," have written this piece myself. to me, the *practice* of Zen meditation is entirely intuitive, while reading or writing about it is mostly intellectual. As for he Shingyo itself, I still feel that one must do one's best to know what a document says before one can decide what it means.

Mind/Spirit: This seems to me to be closer to the Chinese-Japanese intent than "Heart/Mind." There will surely be some controversy over this. See "Un-translated Terms'" above.

A wise person, contemplating the self's existence: This opening of the main text of my "Radical Zen" interpretation is intended to remove the narrative element from the text. "Bosatsu" is used only this one time in the text, though "Bodaisatsu" is used later, perhaps with similar intent. It occurs to me that "Bosatsu," "Bodaisatsu," and "Buddha" may be meant as rankings of enlightened ones.

the meditative state: This is my "Radical Zen" interpretation of *Hannya Haramita,* which is the Japanese phonetic rendering of the Sanskrit *Prajna Paramita*, usually translated as "The highest wisdom."

the five accumulations of experiences which have shaped the mind: Sensory memories, indoctrinations, imaginings, training (as in muscle memory), and thoughts. This is a rendering of *go un.*

rules: In the Sutra, the character *hō* is used in different ways with different possible translations. The dictionaries generally give us "Laws, rules, methods." It is also used to mean *Dharma*.

shotoku: The dictionaries generally give us "income, a living, or profit". I've used "posessions" with the intention of lumping these three words into one convenient one (see note 12, page 30, in Shingyo).

In the midst of emptiness: I read this as meaning "When the mind is deeply in the meditative state," that is to say, "empty," then what follows applies. If "Emptiness" is taken as a supernatural reality it does not.

the three worlds: Some translations call the three worlds those of "Past, Present, and Future". The Dalai Lama says "the three times." Some simply skip the phrase. W. T. Chan gives us the three worlds as those of "Desire, Matter, and Pure Spirit". However, this again presents a supernatural notion. Following here is a different view of it.

If we can think of *shotoku* as a "world," it would be the "material world," that is, a fourth world. We in the West think of these worlds as "Time. Space, Energy, and Matter." An early teacher of mine ignored "Matter," referring only to Time, Space, and Energy, saying that, for us, Time is the foundation of Truth, Space is the foundation of Beauty, and Energy is the foundation of Love. These are the three worlds I prefer.i

Waza, gyō, or *gō.*

This character is not in the text of the sutra, but is crucial in the radical Zen interpretation. It is commonly used to refer to prepared martial arts exercises. In its broadest sense, and in many compound words, it means “action,” “activity,” “feat,” etc. In its *gō* pronunciation, it renders the Sanskrit word, *Karma.*

Karma has a wide variety of meanings, depending on the particular religious or sectarian point of view from which it is being defined. These sometimes involve concepts like “past lives,” “reincarnation,” returning to life in another form,” or some version of “predestination.” A Zen version would, I think, reject all of these notions, and might be stated as, “One’s own actions in the course of one’s lifetime.” This is the interpretation I prefer, because of its insistence on personal responsibility. I would say that this view of it works well in either a meditative, martial arts, or any other context.

悟り

Satori

This character also is not in the text of the sutra. It is made of two parts side by side. The left side means “mind/spirit,” a contraction of the “heart “character. Here it seems to suggest “realizing.” The right side is the ”self” character. The dictionaries give us “Buddhist Enlightenment.” In the Zen context it is used to describe an instantaneous experience of self-knowledge.

視
性

Kensho

Neither are these characters in the text of the sutra. The first one means "to see," the second means "nature." In the Zen context this too is used to describe an instantaneous experience, not so much of self-knowledge, but as the perception of "the nature of Nature."

Closing Note

These two terms are exemplified in the Zen story of a young monk, who says "Ho hum. Before enlightenment, I chopped wood and carried water. After enlightenment, What joy! I chop wood and carry water!"

Notes on the Translations and Commentaries

Boeree, George:

posted on the Internet, 2009 (has a footnote)

This translation is almost certainly based on that of Conze and/or others already in English. He temporizes often. Rather than address the question of the meaning of *shin* in the title, he adds as part of his footnote an interpretive rendering which avoids it. He offers "Avalokiteshvara, the Bodhisattva of Compassion" to render *Kanjizai-bosatsu*, as a way to mediate between the Chinese Kuan-yin and the Sanskrit Avalokiteshvara. He uses "the body" for *shiki*. For *i-mu-shotoku* he uses "no wisdom to attain." His Three Worlds are "past, present, and future," and his *san myaku san bodai* is "full enlightenment." He gives the ending *shu* in Sanskrit, and then translates it as "Gone, gone, gone over, gone fully over. Awakened! So be it!"

The Dalai Lama: *Essence of the Heart Sutra.*

Wisdom Publications, 2005

This book is not focused on the Sutra specifically, but rather uses it as a starting point to expand on Buddhism as a world religion. It gives us many insights into Buddhist philosophy (he is a noted Buddhist scholar), but much more on the Tibetan Buddhist religion (his position is, roughly, that of the Buddhist Pope). The translation into English included is expansive, clearly interpreted from Sanskrit/Tibetan, and reflects this position. One doesn't argue with a Pope or a Dalai Lama.

Deshimaru Taisen: *Mushotoku Mind*

Hohm Press, 2012.

It is my strong impression that this book is intentionally obscurant, but this could be only because this English language version is based on memories of lectures given in France in 1977-78, in Japanese, recorded as notes in French, and again into English. I think it unlikely that it represents the thinking of Deshimaru-*sensei* with any accuracy. The scroll on the front cover reads (more or less) *Mu toku* (the *toku* is incomplete) *kō*, "No profit (or benefit, or attainment), light (or shine, or glitter, *etc*.). The translation of *i-mu-shotoku* in the text gives, "Only the attainment of no attainment."

Haketa,Yoshito: *Kūkai and his Major Works*.

Columbia University Press, 1972, 1984.

Kūkai (774-835) was the founder of the Shingon sect in Japan. The Shingon sect has an esoteric, inner set of teachings called Mikkyō (蜜 教). This book is a translation into English, with many notes and references, of Kūkai's teachings. His discussion of the *Shingyō* is, naturally, esoteric in the extreme.

Hoffman, Djann:

Private publication, ca. 1991.

This version, like that of Boeree, also is almost certainly based on that of Conze and/or others already in English. It translates none of the Sanskrit terms. It avoids the impoverishment implication in *i-mu-shotoku*. Apart from being arranged in verses rather than paragraphs, and a few phrases somewhat more poetic than most, it conforms to Conze, *et al*.

The Lotus in the Flame Temple Liturgy:

Zen Center of Denver, 2001

This version, like that of Boeree and Hoffman, generally conforms to Conze and almost certainly is derived from an earlier translation into English. It uses "Bodhisattva of Compassion" for Kanjizai-*bosatsu*, and uses "attainment too is emptiness" for *i-mu-shotoku*. In other than the title (The Heart Sutra), it does not translate *shin* (心) at all. It reverts to Sanskrit for the *shu*, and does not reprise the abbreviated title.

Mu Soeng Sunim: *Heart Sutra: Ancient Buddhist Wisdom in the Light of Quantum Reality*.

Primary Point Press, 1991.

Mu is a Korean Zen teacher based in Rhode Island. The thrust of this book is the attempt to explore ". . . Emptiness, and its parallels found in the experiments of quantum physics." None of the Sanskrit terms are translated. *I-mu-shotoku* is rendered as "with nothing to attain." He gives "mind" for *shin*.

Stevens, John: *Sacred Calligraphy of the East*.

Shambhala, 1981.

This is a comprehensive study of Asian calligraphy, ranging from the earliest forms of Sanskrit to avant-garde Japanese Zen brushwriting. Its section on the *Shingyō* is thorough and valuable, though with it (as with the other scripts he addresses) the "Manual" section is misleading; one cannot copy the sutra well simply by following instructions in a book, without a previous knowledge of Sino-Japanese and the basic use of the brush.

The included translation, attributed to the San Francisco Zen Center, leaves all the Sanskrit terms un-translated, gives "Indeed, there is nothing to attain" for *i-mu-shotoku*, and uses "mind" for *shin*.

Thich Nhat Hanh: *The Heart of Understanding.*
Parallax Press, 1988, 2009.

Thich is a Vietnamese monk living in France. The translation here avoids the heart/mind question in the title, using the *shin* character to imply the "core" or "essence" of the content. It gives "Because there is no attainment" for *i-mu-shotoku*. *Shin* is "mind" in the following sentence. The ending *shu* remains in Sanskrit, but is translated in a footnote as "Gone, gone, gone all the way over, everyone gone to the other shore, enlightment, Hurrah!"

Van Ghelue, Nadja: *The Heart Sutra in Calligraphy.*
Stone Bridge Press, 2009.

This gives us a unique, personal, artist's view of the text. It includes her own excellent calligraphic rendering of it, in the seldom-used style called "lesser seal script," similar to a version in a book by Harada Rokujisai Kampō. Like Stevens, it includes instructions for writing the sutra. The included translation, un-attributed, leaves all the Sanskrit terms un-translated, gives "Indeed, there is nothing to attain" for *i-mu-shotoku*, and uses "mind" for *shin*.

The Hermit and the Shingyō

The legend of the original transmission from Gautama Buddha to the first patriarch of the Zen sect says that it occurred with not one word, just a smile and the passing of one flower. Since then, it is said that the transmission has continued unbroken, outside the sutras, without "Mudra, Mantra, or Mandala" (mystical hand positions, incantations, or sacred objects).

In our time, Katagiri-*roshi* wrote a book he called *You Have to Say Something*. It would appear that in following the Zen tradition as described, the truly enlightened one would not have to say anything at all. It seems, however, that I, the hermit, like Katagiri-*roshi,* must.

This ageing hermit both chants and writes the *Shingyō* nearly every day, with the goal of writing it (and any other calligraphic text he undertakes) beautifully, and from memory. Daily practice as an approach to art began with the classical guitar, transferred itself to the martial arts, and persists in his study of the brush. He practices religiously, but he doesn't think of it as a religious practice. He has read commentaries on the *Shingyō* and histories of it and translations of it in both English and Japanese. He thinks he knows it fairly well by now.

He lives in ordinary, practical, humanly-measured time, as well as in the elastic time of time-space, even perhaps in ultimate timelessness. In ordinary, practical, humanly-measured time, the sort with a past, a present and a future, he has lived and worked for the last quarter-century in a house on a forested mountainside. He is visited there by birds and squirrels and chipmunks and foxes and deer and elk and occasionally a bear. He loves them all. They are his most profound teachers. They force him to ask himself the most difficult, childlike questions, and have convinced him that one can never know the world so long as one holds to the idea that the human has greater value in it than any other living thing. He knows that each of these teachers sees the world differently, some acutely color-sensitive, others attuned to shape or scent or sound or movement. He also sees that all of them always, *always*, pay very close attention. He hopes he is learning that from them.

He knows that sometimes he does pay very close attention, and when he does, it sometimes leads to *satori. Satori* is what he thinks of as a Zen version of epiphany. He has had several such experiences. They have led him to the knowledge that he is he and not he, he is I and not I, and in some way he is you and not you. There are certain things one can learn only in schools. There are other things one can only learn out in the world, in society. There are also things one can only learn in hermitage. This seems to be one of those.

He has practiced Zen for a long time. He has no *dharmas*, nothing that is "held to", no beliefs (well, he has at least one. It embarrasses him, but he can't seem to exorcize it: He believes that the world exists whether he's there to perceive it or not. There may be others as yet unidentified. Oh, shame!). This is not to say he lacks commitments. He just doesn't consider beliefs to be necessary to sustaining them.

Is the *Shingyō* a cosmological statement rather than an epistemological or psychological one? It has been pointed out to him that cosmology and epistemology may well not be two distinct sciences; that there may well be no difference at all between them. It may be that quantum physicists are in fact dealing with inquiries in which a distinction no longer exists between cosmology and epistemology, or that the line between them has become thoroughly blurred. Either way, I am delighted to hear that quantum physicists are inspired by Zen thought and practice. Still, I can't help thinking of this as something of a digression at best, because they believe that, as Stephen Hawking put it (in *A Brief History of Time*): ". . . the universe is governed by a set of rational laws that we can discover and understand." Another statement of belief from a physicist, Philip R. Wallace, in his book, *Paradox Lost*, says, "Science involves belief in the objective reality of the world of our experience . . . ." These beliefs will necessarily and immediately impose themselves upon all of their insights, requiring them to conform to their terms, and so will render them penultimate, divesting them of their potential to reveal anything of Ultimate reality.

Human life *almost* always goes on in the penultimate reality of practical, humanly-measured time, space, energy, matter. It only pops out of it in certain anomalous situations, like miracles, the appearances of ghosts, ESP events, telekinesis, certain practices in the martial and other arts related to *chi* (気 *ki* in Japanese), that sort of thing.

Life *always* goes on in Ultimate reality, even in cases such as these. I think that the author of the *Shingyō* knew this, and wrote it in the hope of urging his readers to pay attention to the reality where life *always* goes on.

Robert Bellah, in his *Tokugawa Religion*, points out that the modes of belief in Buddhist deities can be placed on a continuum between complete transcendence and complete immanence, that is, that deities are all "out there", existing independently of our perception (as in the Pure Land sect) and, in the case of the most radical Zen sects, that they are all "in here", where they are seen as metaphoric of human mental states or experiences, and existing in no other way.

Implicit in the radical Zen sects' rejection of transcendent deities is the idea that everything thought, or even perceived, is created in and by the mind; that not only deities, but *all things*, exist solely as mental constructs. Carried to its extreme, this would have to include also the categories of our perception: time, space, energy, matter, and all their sub-categories. It is not that these categories do not exist, but that they are demonstrably inventions of the human mind, and cannot be proven to exist independently of it.

In China, this thesis goes back to pre-Christian and pre-Buddhist times. When this position is taken in Western philosophy it is called Solipsism, and dismissed entirely. Hawking states that ". . . order in the mind causes disorder elsewhere," and says that disorder equals death. I find this an interesting idea, one that seems to support the Solipsist view from a quantum physicist's perspective. This hermit finds himself unable to carry his perception quite so far, and so is left with his one, pesky *dharma*: His belief that the world exists whether or not he's here to perceive it.

He remains uncertain whether the author of the *Shingyō* did so or not. He wonders if the bodhisattva is one who stops short of complete Solipsism (in order to save all living things), and the Buddha is one who actually goes there (that is to say, to Nirvana). He wonders if the *Shingyō* can answer that question for him; certainly nothing else he has read on either Buddhism or Solipsism has been able to do so. In any case, he knows that ordinary, practical, humanly-measurable time is not ultimately real, nor are humanly-measured space, energy, matter.

The truly enlightened one would not have to say anything. It seems, however, that I, or perhaps not I, must, having started, try to say it all. I know this is fraught with danger. One can well appear to be a proselytizer, a preacher, a salesman of beliefs. I intend to be nothing of the sort.

The chanting, copying, or translating of the *Shingyō* does not necessarily lead to Solipsism or hermitage. On the contrary, such exercises may lead to a new way to examine the workings of the mind, and perhaps the world, and even, perhaps, one's idea of the universe. It has done so for me and not me. May it do so for you and not you.

M.J. Sullivan
Tōshoin, 2011

A Final and Fanciful Note on the Authorship of the Shingyō

As I mentioned in the Introduction, some scholars and historians think that the *Shingyō* was actually written in Chinese originally, and that the Sanskrit and Tibetan versions were translated *from the Chinese,* rather than the other way around (see Janice Nattier, The Nattier Hypothesis). Although I love that idea, I decided to ignore it in the main text and followed the conventional wisdom instead. This has been bothering me ever since, so I have put together this little fable, based on the notion that those scholars and historians were right, and on the inspiration of the Ox-Herding Pictures of Kuo-an Shih-yuan (Kakuan Shian in Japanese). These pictures symbolize the stages of Buddhist enlightenment; this story is based mainly on the sixth one. Readers may also note references to the Zen stories "I chop wood and carry water" and "One robe, one bowl."

A young monk named Wu, as he chopped wood and carried water for the monastery, was constantly troubled by thoughts of deities. He would look up at the sky and wonder how Shariputra and Avalokitesvara and all the ten-thousand bodhisattvas and the ten-thousand demons could live up there? And if they really do, why can't I see them?

Once a week, after evening meditation in the great hall, it was his turn to meet privately with the master to talk about his practice. "Why do we name Avalokitesvara as Kuan-Yin?" he would ask.

"Just because," the master would say. "Stop asking."

"Why did the Buddha think Shariputra was his best disciple?" he would ask.

"Just because," the master would say. "Stop asking."

But Wu could not stop asking. The ten-thousand bodhisattvas and the ten-thousand demons stalked him as he chopped wood and carried water and meditated and ate his brown rice and pickles and relieved himself and even as he slept. "Ignore them," the master would say. "Stop asking."

"In the dharma lectures you talk about them all the time," Wu said, "and the sutras that you read to us are filled with them. How can I ignore them?"

"Stop asking."

This continued for some years. Wu was always beaten with the paddle during meditation, not because he would fall asleep, but because the master could see that his mind was filled with the ten-thousand bodhisattvas and the ten-thousand demons.

Finally the master gave up on Wu. "You are learning nothing here. Go out into the world and beg."

So Wu, wrapped in his one robe and carrying his one wooden bowl, left the monastery that very night and walked out into the world in his tattered sandals, with no idea how or where or from whom to beg.

A road meandered through the forests and fields and mountain passes, and Wu followed it for a time in the dark, pursued relentlessly by the ten-thousand bodhisattvas and the ten-thousand demons. Soon he tired, curled himself up in his one robe and, using his wooden bowl as a pillow, slept beneath a tall tree not far from the road.

Birdsong woke him before full light. He turned over and tried to sleep some more, but a squirrel began to chatter angrily at him. "Get away from my tree, you big animal! Get away! Get away!"

Wu gathered himself and straightened his robe and picked up his bowl and stumbled stiffly away from the tree. "Farther!" the squirrel said. "Hit the road!" As a silent protest, Wu relieved himself on the tree before he left.

Most Chinese people of that time did not like beggars, especially those with shaven heads and orange robes who had forsaken family and ancestors, so the few passersby shunned him as he walked, his hunger increasing as the sun made its way upward. Near mid-day his stomach no longer rumbled, but roared. When he came upon another tree, he chased off a squirrel and gathered a few of the nuts scattered under the tree and cracked them and ate them. Fortunately, a brook ran by not far from the tree, and he filled his bowl from it and drank and washed his face in it. Then he sat, resting under the tree, trying to feel like the Buddha. That didn't work, so instead he watched the few passersby on the road.

Most of them were on foot. An occasional horseman passed, an occasional cart drawn by a donkey. He drifted into a half-sleep as the day warmed, but wakened to the sound of hooves. Not a horse's hooves, those of some other animal. Then he heard, faintly, the sound of a flute. He stood to get a better look.

Now, Wu had spent most of his life in the monastery, but even from there, when he went out to chop wood or carry water, he saw people and animals in the forest or on the road, and had some idea of the life outside. Never before, however, had he seen a man riding on an ox, with no saddle or reins, playing a flute. That was what he saw that day from the side of the road.

When the man and the ox came to where Wu was standing, they paused. The man stopped playing the flute and looked at Wu and smiled. The ox turned his head and looked at Wu and, in the only way an ox can, smiled too. Wu was too surprised by this to smile, he could just stand staring.

After a few minutes of that, the man on the ox beckoned to Wu to come closer. The ox gently tossed his head with what appeared to be a similar invitation. Wu shook off his trance and walked carefully onto the road. There was no one else in sight. When the young monk got close enough, the man spoke to him.

"You do not like begging," the man said.

"I'm no good at it," Wu said, hanging his head.

"That's because you don't like doing it. Would you consider taking a job instead?"

Wu considered very briefly, then said, "All I know how to do is chop wood and carry water and recite parts of a few sutras."

"Then you will learn something new. Once in a while Ox will have to leave some droppings, fouling this fine road. He doesn't mean to do it, but, being an ox, he can't help it. If you follow behind us, and collect his droppings in your bowl, and spread them near the roots of the trees we pass, at the end of the day we will lead you to water in which to wash your bowl and yourself, and we will give you food and safe places to rest as we proceed on our journey of ten-thousand *li*."

Ox then dropped a small pile onto the road, as a sample. Wu was surprised by its sweet, grassy smell. He collected the pile with his hands, put it in his bowl, carried it to the tree under which he'd been resting just moments before, and spread it around the roots. Birds twittered and flittered in the tree. A squirrel made an amazing leap to a lower branch and smiled at Wu, who smiled back at the squirrel. Then, still smiling, he walked back to the man and the ox and smiled at them and said, "I'll take the job."

The man smiled back, resumed his flute playing. Ox resumed his leisurely pace, and Wu followed, enjoying the music. Now and then Ox would stop and leave a deposit on the road (always near a tree). Wu would scoop the droppings up into his bowl, and spread them under the nearby tree. Birds would twitter and flitter. A squirrel would perform an amazing acrobatic feat and smile at him. Then Ox would resume his leisurely pace and the man would play another song on his flute.

Just as the sun withdrew behind a mountain, Ox turned off the road and ambled into the forest. Soon they reached a clear pool under a gentle waterfall, where the man dismounted and Ox drank and Wu cleaned his bowl and himself, then gathered some sticks and dried grass and laid a fire where the man had told him. Ox wandered into the nearby meadow and grazed. The man disappeared, but soon returned with a bag of brown rice and some vegetables, which he and Wu ate, sitting under a large, leafy tree.

This pattern continued for many, even countless, days. Wu's hair grew longer and longer. Each time Ox left droppings not far from a tree, Wu collected them and spread them under the tree and birds twittered and flittered, and a squirrel performed an amazing acrobatic feat and smiled at him. One day, many, even countless, days later, the man disappeared, but soon returned and gave Wu a new robe and fresh sandals. Later, after he and Wu ate, sitting under yet another large, leafy tree, the man spoke.

"Our journey of ten-thousand *li* is nearly over," he said. "Ox and I will soon be home, and you will find a fine place for yourself, where you will write the most beloved sutra of all."

And so it happened. The man reached home. Ox retired to a particularly lush, green meadow. Wu retreated to a cave, where all the birds and the squirrels, whose trees he had fertilized with droppings from dear old Ox, brought him food, and the birds entertained him with song and the squirrels with amazing acrobatic feats. They also brought him fibers from the mulberry to make paper, charcoal to make ink, young shoots of bamboo to make handles for binding tufts of his long hair (now entirely gray) into writing brushes. With these he wrote the famous and beloved Heart Sutra, in which he re-named Avalokitesvara as Kuan-Tzu-Ts'ai, and which even the Tibetan and Indian Buddhists loved so much they added it to their canon on first reading. These many centuries later, we still copy and chant and quote it, thanks to Ox, and to the man who played the flute while riding the ox, and to the outcast monk called Wu.

Tōshoin, 2014

Selected Bibilography of References in English

Bellah, Robert: *Tokugawa Religions.*
The Free Press, 1985.

Brown, Sid: *The journey of One Buddhist Nun.*
State University of New York, 2001.

Chan Wing-Tsit: *A Souce Book in Chinese Philosophy.*
Princeton University Press, 1963.

Chen, Janey: *A Practical English-Chinese Pronouncing Dictionary.*
Tuttle, 1970.

Deshimaru Taisen: *Mushotoku Mind.*
(Based on the translation by Ilsa Fatt) Hohm Press, 2012.

Goodrich, Chauncey: *Chinese-English Pocket Dictionary.*
Hong Kong University Press, 1965.

Hagen, Steve: *How the World Can Be the Way It Is.*
Quest Books, 1995.

——————: *Buddhism Plain and Simple.*
Tuttle, 1997.

Hawking, Stephen: *A Brief History of Time.*
Bantam, 1988.

Haketa,Yoshito: *Kūkai and his Major Works.*
Columbia University Press, 1972, 1984.

Jung C.G.: *Psychology and Religion,* and others, Trns. R.F.C. Hull.
Princeton, 1967.

Kaifeng: *A Modern Chinese-English Dictionary.*
Oxford University Press, 1960.

Kapleau: *The Three Pillars of Zen.*
Beacon Press, 1967.

Katagiri Dainin: *You Have to Say Something.*
Shambhala, 1998.

Kawamoto, et al: *The Kodansha English-Japanese Dictionary.*
Kodansha, 1969.

Kodansha Encyclopedia of Japan.
Kodansha, 1983.

Miyamoto Musashi (Victor Harris, Trans.): *A Book of Five Rings.*
Overlook Press, 1974.

Mu Soeng Sunim: *Heart Sutra: Ancient Buddhist Wisdom in the Light of Quantum Reality.*
Primary Point Press, 1991.

Nelson, Andrew N.: *The Modern Reader's Japanese-English Character Dictionary.*
Tuttle, 1984.

Northrop, F.S.C.: *The Logic of the Sciences and the Humanities.*
Macmillan, 1948.

Stevens, John: *Sacred Calligraphy of the East.*
Shambhala, 1981.

Sullivan, M.J.: *Seihō's Kanji Workbook.*
Asian Humanities Press, 1991.

Suzuki: *What Is Zen?*
Perennial Library, 1972

Takahashi Morio: *Romanized English-Japanese Japanese-English Dictionary.* Taiseido, 1953.

Thich Nhat Hanh: *The Heart of Understannding.* Parallax Press, 1988, 2009.

Tillich, Paul: *Theology of Culture* (and other works) Oxford University Press, 1959.

Van Ghelue, Nadja: *The Heart Sutra in Callligraphy.* Stone Bridge Press, 2009.

Wallace, Philip R.: *Paradox Lost.* Springer, 1996.

Welch, Holmes: *Taoism: the Parting of the Way.* Beacon Press, 1957, 1965.

Yagyū Munenori: *Heihōkadensho* (William Scott Wilson, Trans.) Kodansha, 2003

Victoria, Brian Daizen: *Zen at War.* Rowman and Littlefield, 2006.

Acknowledgements

I must begin with a statement of deep gratitude to Richard Hill and Sakurada Yuhei, who pointed me toward Japan through Zen and the martial arts, and who are no longer here to read this.

Once I actually got to Japan I had many teachers and guides. It would be entirely true to say that I learned from everyone in Takamatsu, but especially from the great swordsmen, Morikawa Gembu-*sensei* and Iwata Norikazu-*sensei*, the great calligrapher, Komori Shiun-*sensei*, and all the fine teachers of Takamatsu Daiichi Koto Gakko. All my thanks to you always.

I owe a great deal to Asakawa Junko-*sensei* and Takemori Tsuyoshi-*sensei*, or Nippon Shuji Kyoiku Zaidan, who introduced me to Harada Rokujisai Kampō and his sons, Shokei and Hiroshi. They taught me so much, and were my kind hosts at the Kampō Kaikan in Kyoto. I can never thank them enough.

Perhaps my greatest debt in terms of this particular work is to Dr. Charles W. Swain. On my return from Japan, I felt I had to "learn what I had learned" there. At the time, Dr. Swain was the head of the Asian Studies Program at the Florida State University and accepted me as his graduate assistant. He introduced me to a vast array of literature, showed me how to read it with discrimination, and has been a valuable teacher, critic, and friend ever since. He was kind enough to write the Foreword to *Shingyō*, and argued and encouraged me through the writing process to the end. Many thanks to you, sir.

Dr. Swain also gave me the opportunity to co-teach a class in East Asian Humanities with Dr. Winston Lo, who taught me a great deal. Many thanks to Djann Hoffman for letting me use his translation in *Shingyō*.

Near the end of writing this, Dr. Jun Shan was of great help in clarifying points I'd missed or had misrepresented out of ignorance of the Chinese tradition. Any remaining errors are, of course, my own.

Thanks, as always, are due to Jim Horne Minter, friend, literary advisor and publisher, for his constant support of all my work. Thanks to Nancy Mack and Jim Minter Jr. as well, whose computer skills turned a manuscript into an actual printed book.

And ever as always, to my beloved Herta, all love and gratitude. She lives it with few words, but in a plethora of flowers.

Author photo courtesy Colorado Academy of Martial Arts

M. J. Sullivan has a BA in Humanities and an MA in Asian Studies. *WAZA*, his first novel about Japanese Buddhism and the martial arts, received the CoVisions Recognition Award for Literature.

He earned the name Seihō and his teacher's license in calligraphy from Harada Kampō, founder of Nippon Shuji Kyōiku Zaidan. He also wrote the English language versions of their textbooks. He was made an Honorary Citizen of Takamatsu and one year was the *nidan* level swordsmanship champion of Kagawa Prefecture.

Deeply involved with Zen and Japanese culture, he paints and writes at Tōshoin (洞 書 院, Cave Writing Hall), his studio in the Colorado Rocky Mountains.

SILVERBACK SAGES, PUBLISHERS

Shingyō: Reflections on Translating the Heart Sutra
by M. J. Sullivan
(Seihō)

For readers who appreciate fine writing and challenging questions, we also publish by the same author.

In This Living Body
by M. J. Sullivan

In which Sullivan weaves romance and mystery into this novel about the spiritual testing of a young American in a highly-secret order of Japanese monks.

Both books are available directly from the publisher at:

www.silverbacksages.com

And from:

amazon.com

Direct Publisher discounts are offered to educational institutions, any *zendō* or *dōjō*, bookstores, and on all orders for five or more copies.

Bookstores may also purchase directly from Ingram.

Silverback Sages, Publishers, L.L.C. was licensed in Northern New Mexico in early 2011.